Ghost Hunting

EVP
LOG BOOK

Book Published by
Lee Steer
Founder of project-reveal.
This is a paranormal
investigation team, based
in south Yorkshire.
www.project-reveal.com

www.facebook.com/projectr
eveal

Publisher of various
paranormal books, and
certified Android App
Developer

EVP Log book is like a diary were you log your findings as you go.

All organized, in one place.

Log Instruction Page:

This page contains instructions for completing this log book. Each entry is covered in the order it appears. There are three pages of entries for each investigation. Details for each are given.

Set Up Sheet

The Set Up Sheet is intended to provide a record of the configuration used in this investigation. The equipment used is recorded here at the start of the investigation. Additionally the location of all fixed monitoring points should be logged. If during the course of the investigation the equipment is moved or repositioned a second set up sheet should be completed for that configuration. Two Logs are provided on each page. If additional set ups are made, print additional Set Up sheets as needed.

Line 1 – Audio Equipment Used. These lines are to record the equipment used in this investigation. Include all audio hardware directly used in the area under surveillance. Include mikes, recorders, mixers, dynamic EMF sensors, cameras with audio recording capabilities etc. The make and model of each should be recorded for each if applicable.

Line 2 – Support Equipment Used. These lines are to list any equipment used in the area but not directly related to the EVP study. This would include such items as Static EMFmonitors, cameras without audio capabilities, proximity detectors, etc.

Line 3 – Sources of Interaction. This list is a place for a record to be made of anything noted that might be the source of a false EVP. The location should be examined and anything present which might cause noise, create electromagnetic fields, generate vibrations, etc. should be noted here. This would include nearby highways, motors, televisions in adjacent rooms, furnaces and air conditioning, computers, etc. If possible these devices should be turned off, but if that cannot be accomplished they should be logged here and the investigator should be aware that they could create false EVP.

Line 4 – Layout of Target Area. This area of the page is left clear so the investigator can make a sketch of where the equipment is located in the target area. If multiple rooms are covered simultaneously, draw the floor plan of each and show approximately the location of the mikes, detectors, and any other equipment positioned in the target area. If applicable also show the location of the recording and control point. Include items such as proximity sensors and cameras if they are placed in the target area.

2

Real Time Log Sheet

The Real Time Log Sheet is intended to provide a running log of all events once the monitoring session is underway. There are four columns on this page, they are Line, Time, Event, and Witnessed. The "Line" entry is intended to simply provide a sequential numbering system to each entry of the entire log. The "Time entry is to log the time of the event. Record the nature of the event on the "Event" Line. Finally, the investigator who witnessed or caused the event should initial the entry under the "Witness" column. All events related to this session should be logged whether or not they are unexplained This includes things such as tape changes, EMF activation, etc. If the equipment is reconfigured, then a new Set Up sheet and Real Time Log should be made for the new locations..

Post Investigation EVP Summary Sheet

This page is completed after the field investigation has been completed. Any recording made is evaluated and any EVP captured is isolated from the original tapes. The EVP is graded in accordance with the factors given in the Grading Outline. Any EVP heard is logged on this page according to the time recorded on the Real Time Sheet. There is room for three entries on each Summary Sheet. If more is needed include additional pages

Enter the Time, Classification, and Type of processing applied (if any) on the first line.

Record your impression of what the EVP is saying on the second line.

If any external stimuli were applied such as an EM Field to cause a reaction in the area list that here. If the EVP is in answer to a question you asked, or a response to a conversation, record your question on this line.

Other sounds recorded is a place to list those extraneous noises that might be mistaken for something else. Motors starting, traffic, or phones ringing are among the things that would be logged here.

1

REPORTING INVESTIGATOR NAME OR NUMBER:_____

~ EVP Log Book ~

URN: _____ , _____ , _____ - _____ - _____

Day Month Year Number Type

Location :

_____

Investigating Team : _____

_____

_____

_____

_____

Set Up Sheet - Hardware Configuration

Audio Equipment ----- _____

_____

_____

_____

_____

Support Equipment -- _____

_____

_____

Sources of Interaction - _____

_____

_____

Audio Equipment ----- _____

_____

_____

_____

Support Equipment -- _____

_____

_____

_____

Sources of Interaction - _____

_____

_____

_____

3___

Layout of Target Area - (Sketch Below)

Real Time Event Log 4___
Line Time Event Witnessed

_____ - _____ -

_____

_____ - _____

_____ - _____ -

_____

_____ - _____

_____ - _____ -

_____

_____ - _____

_____ - _____ -

_____

_____ - _____

_____ - _____ -

_____

_____ - _____

_____ - _____ -

_____

_____ - _____

_____ - _____ -

_____

_____ - _____

Quality Grading: (EVP Research Standards)

- o **A_** Heard and understood clearly without any signal processing at all, Like a normal voice.
- o **B_** Processed using analog filtering, but most who hear it can decipher the content. There is little disagreement on what is recorded.
- o **C_** Processed using analog filtering, but still hard to hear. Potential for disagreement on content.
- o **D_** Digital processing employed to make out anything at all. Disagreement over content, some may not hear anything.
- o **E_** Most hear nothing; some may claim to hear a voice. Processing may result in different messages being heard.

Content Grading

- o **1_** Easily related to surroundings. For instance: A soldier who was killed mentioning the battle, etc.
- o **2_** Unrelated but meaningful, such as a statement "I love you". Could be for anyone or maybe no one present.
- o **3_** Gibberish. Meaningless groups of words but still recognizable as words or phrases.
- o **4_** Utterances. Vocalized sounds not words. Includes grunts and groans. Before classifying here make sure you are not dealing with a foreign language which should actually be in categories 1-3.
- o **5_** Non vocal sounds. Thumps Bangs, Pops, Footsteps, etc.

Source Grading: 5

- o **M_** Multiple voices heard, unable to differentiate.
- o **U_** The gender or age cannot be determined.
- o **W_** The voice is clearly that of a child.
- o **X_** The voice is clearly that of a woman.
- o **Y_** The voice is clearly that of a man.
- o **Z_** The recording is of an animal sound (Barking, Meowing, Vocalizations only)

- Note that many EVPs may contain portions falling into multiple categories. Parts may be clear then fade out. Vocalizations may be preceded or followed by non-vocal sounds. Thus a particular EVP may have multiple classifications. If you are classifying the overall EVP, use the most predominate characteristics.

To Grade your EVP, select the appropriate **letter** from the first column, **number** from the second column and finally **letter** from the third. Enter that grading under the "Classification" on the Post Investigation Summary Sheet.

Post Investigation Summary Sheet 6__

Time : _____ Classification: _____ Processing Applied? No ___ Yes ___ (Type) _____

Transcript :
_____
_____

Any external stimuli applied? No _____ Yes _____ (Type)
_____
_____

Leading Questions or Conversation
_____
_____

Any other sounds recorded?
_____Reviewed
By: _____, _____.

Time : _____ **Classification:** _____ **Processing Applied? No**
___ **Yes** ___ **(Type)** _____

Transcript :
_____
_____

Any external stimuli applied? No ____ **Yes** ____ **(Type)**
_____
_____

Leading Questions or Conversation
_____
_____

Any other sounds recorded?
_____**Reviewed**
By: _____, _____

Time : _____ **Classification:** _____ **Processing Applied? No**
___ **Yes** ___ **(Type)** _____

Transcript :
_____
_____

Any external stimuli applied? No ____ **Yes** ____ **(Type)**
_____
_____

Leading Questions or Conversation
_____
_____

Any other sounds recorded?
_____**Reviewed**
By: _____, _____

1

**REPORTING INVESTIGATOR NAME OR
NUMBER:**_____

~ EVP Log Book ~

URN: _____ , _____ , _____ - _____ - _____

Day Month Year Number Type

Location :

_____

Investigating Team : _____

_____

_____

_____

_____

Set Up Sheet - Hardware Configuration

Audio Equipment ----- _____

_____

_____

_____

_____

Support Equipment -- _____

_____

_____

Sources of Interaction - _____

_____

_____

Audio Equipment ----- _____

_____

_____

_____

Support Equipment -- _____ _____

_____

_____

_____

Sources of Interaction - _____ _____

_____

_____

_____

3___

Layout of Target Area - (Sketch Below)

Real Time Event Log 4___
Line Time Event Witnessed

_____ - _____ -

_____

_____ - _____

_____ - _____ -

_____ - _____

_____ - _____ -

_____ - _____

_____ - _____ -

_____ - _____

_____ - _____ -

_____ - _____

_____ - _____ -

_____ - _____

_____ - _____ -

_____ - _____

_____ - _____ -

_____ - _____

_____ - _____ -

_____ - _____

Quality Grading: (EVP Research Standards)

- o **A_** Heard and understood clearly without any signal processing at all, Like a normal voice.
- o **B_** Processed using analog filtering, but most who hear it can decipher the content. There is little disagreement on what is recorded.
- o **C_** Processed using analog filtering, but still hard to hear. Potential for disagreement on content.
- o **D_** Digital processing employed to make out anything at all. Disagreement over content, some may not hear anything.
- o **E_** Most hear nothing; some may claim to hear a voice. Processing may result in different messages being heard.

Content Grading

- o **1_** Easily related to surroundings. For instance: A soldier who was killed mentioning the battle, etc.
- o **2_** Unrelated but meaningful, such as a statement "I love you". Could be for anyone or maybe no one present.
- o **3_** Gibberish. Meaningless groups of words but still recognizable as words or phrases.
- o **4_** Utterances. Vocalized sounds not words. Includes grunts and groans. Before classifying here make sure you are not dealing with a foreign language which should actually be in categories 1-3.
- o **5_** Non vocal sounds. Thumps Bangs, Pops, Footsteps, etc.

Source Grading: 5

- o **M_** Multiple voices heard, unable to differentiate.
- o **U_** The gender or age cannot be determined.
- o **W_** The voice is clearly that of a child.
- o **X_** The voice is clearly that of a woman.
- o **Y_** The voice is clearly that of a man.
- o **Z_** The recording is of an animal sound (Barking, Meowing, Vocalizations only)

- Note that many EVPs may contain portions falling into multiple categories. Parts may be clear then fade out. Vocalizations may be preceded or followed by non-vocal sounds. Thus a particular EVP may have multiple classifications. If you are classifying the overall EVP, use the most predominate characteristics.

To Grade your EVP, select the appropriate **letter** from the first column, **number** from the second column and finally **letter** from the third. Enter that grading under the "Classification" on the Post Investigation Summary Sheet.

Post Investigation Summary Sheet 6__

Time : _____ **Classification:** _____ **Processing Applied? No** ___ **Yes** ___ **(Type)** _____

Transcript :
_____
_____

Any external stimuli applied? No _____ **Yes** _____ **(Type)**
_____
_____

Leading Questions or Conversation
_____
_____

Any other sounds recorded?
_____**Reviewed**
By: _____, _____

Time : _____ Classification: _____ Processing Applied? No ___ Yes ___ (Type) _____

Transcript :

_____

_____

Any external stimuli applied? No ____ Yes ____ (Type)

_____

_____

Leading Questions or Conversation

_____

_____

Any other sounds recorded?

_____Reviewed By: _____, _____

Time : _____ Classification: _____ Processing Applied? No ___ Yes ___ (Type) _____

Transcript :

_____

_____

Any external stimuli applied? No ____ Yes ____ (Type)

_____

_____

Leading Questions or Conversation

_____

_____

Any other sounds recorded?

_____Reviewed By: _____, _____

REPORTING INVESTIGATOR NAME OR NUMBER:_____

~ EVP Log Book ~

URN: _____ , _____ , _____ - _____ - _____

Day Month Year Number Type

Location :

_____

Investigating Team : _____

_____

_____

_____

_____

Set Up Sheet - Hardware Configuration

Audio Equipment ----- _____

_____

_____

_____

_____

Support Equipment -- _____

_____

_____

Sources of Interaction - _____

_____

_____

Audio Equipment ----- _____

_____

_____

_____

Support Equipment -- _____

_____

_____

_____

Sources of Interaction - _____

_____

_____

_____

3___

Layout of Target Area - (Sketch Below)

Real Time Event Log 4___
Line Time Event Witnessed

_____ - _____ - _____

_____

_____ - _____

_____ - _____ - _____

_____

_____ - _____

_____ - _____ - _____

_____

_____ - _____

_____ - _____ - _____

_____

_____ - _____

_____ - _____ - _____

_____

_____ - _____

_____ - _____ - _____

_____

_____ - _____

_____ - _____ - _____

_____

_____ - _____

_____ - _____ - _____

_____

_____ - _____

Quality Grading: (EVP Research Standards)

- **A_** Heard and understood clearly without any signal processing at all, Like a normal voice.
- **B_** Processed using analog filtering, but most who hear it can decipher the content. There is little disagreement on what is recorded.
- **C_** Processed using analog filtering, but still hard to hear. Potential for disagreement on content.
- **D_** Digital processing employed to make out anything at all. Disagreement over content, some may not hear anything.
- **E_** Most hear nothing; some may claim to hear a voice. Processing may result in different messages being heard.

Content Grading

- **1_** Easily related to surroundings. For instance: A soldier who was killed mentioning the battle, etc.
- **2_** Unrelated but meaningful, such as a statement "I love you". Could be for anyone or maybe no one present.
- **3_** Gibberish. Meaningless groups of words but still recognizable as words or phrases.
- **4_** Utterances. Vocalized sounds not words. Includes grunts and groans. Before classifying here make sure you are not dealing with a foreign language which should actually be in categories 1-3.
- **5_** Non vocal sounds. Thumps Bangs, Pops, Footsteps, etc.

Source Grading: 5

- **M_** Multiple voices heard, unable to differentiate.
- **U_** The gender or age cannot be determined.
- **W_** The voice is clearly that of a child.
- **X_** The voice is clearly that of a woman.
- **Y_** The voice is clearly that of a man.
- **Z_** The recording is of an animal sound (Barking, Meowing, Vocalizations only)

- Note that many EVPs may contain portions falling into multiple categories. Parts may be clear then fade out. Vocalizations may be preceded or followed by non-vocal sounds. Thus a particular EVP may have multiple classifications. If you are classifying the overall EVP, use the most predominate characteristics.

To Grade your EVP, select the appropriate **letter** from the first column, **number** from the second column and finally **letter** from the third. Enter that grading under the "Classification" on the Post Investigation Summary Sheet.

Post Investigation Summary Sheet 6__

Time : _____ Classification: _____ Processing Applied? No ___ Yes ___ (Type) _____

Transcript :
_____
_____

Any external stimuli applied? No ____ Yes ____ (Type)
_____
_____

Leading Questions or Conversation
_____
_____

Any other sounds recorded?
_____Reviewed
By: _____, _____

Time : _____ **Classification:** _____ **Processing Applied? No**
___ **Yes** ___ **(Type)** _____

Transcript :
_____
_____

Any external stimuli applied? No ____ **Yes** ____ **(Type)**
_____
_____

Leading Questions or Conversation
_____
_____

Any other sounds recorded?
_____**Reviewed**
By: _____, _____

Time : _____ **Classification:** _____ **Processing Applied? No**
___ **Yes** ___ **(Type)** _____

Transcript :
_____
_____

Any external stimuli applied? No ____ **Yes** ____ **(Type)**
_____
_____

Leading Questions or Conversation
_____
_____

Any other sounds recorded?
_____**Reviewed**
By: _____, _____

1

**REPORTING INVESTIGATOR NAME OR
NUMBER:**_____

~ EVP Log Book ~

URN: _____ , _____ , _____ - _____ - _____

Day Month Year Number Type

Location :

_____

Investigating Team : _____

_____

_____

_____

_____

Set Up Sheet - Hardware Configuration

Audio Equipment ----- _____

_____

_____

_____

_____

Support Equipment -- _____

_____

_____

Sources of Interaction - _____

_____

_____

Audio Equipment ----- _____

_____

_____

_____

Support Equipment -- _____

_____

_____

_____

Sources of Interaction - _____

_____

_____

_____

3___

Layout of Target Area - (Sketch Below)

Real Time Event Log 4___
Line Time Event Witnessed

_____ - _____ -
_____
_____ - _____

_____ - _____ -
_____
_____ - _____

_____ - _____ -
_____
_____ - _____

_____ - _____ -
_____
_____ - _____

_____ - _____ -
_____
_____ - _____

_____ - _____ -
_____
_____ - _____

_____ - _____ -
_____
_____ - _____

Quality Grading: (EVP Research Standards)

- **A_** Heard and understood clearly without any signal processing at all, Like a normal voice.
- **B_** Processed using analog filtering, but most who hear it can decipher the content. There is little disagreement on what is recorded.
- **C_** Processed using analog filtering, but still hard to hear. Potential for disagreement on content.
- **D_** Digital processing employed to make out anything at all. Disagreement over content, some may not hear anything.
- **E_** Most hear nothing; some may claim to hear a voice. Processing may result in different messages being heard.

Content Grading

- **1_** Easily related to surroundings. For instance: A soldier who was killed mentioning the battle, etc.
- **2_** Unrelated but meaningful, such as a statement "I love you". Could be for anyone or maybe no one present.
- **3_** Gibberish. Meaningless groups of words but still recognizable as words or phrases.
- **4_** Utterances. Vocalized sounds not words. Includes grunts and groans. Before classifying here make sure you are not dealing with a foreign language which should actually be in categories 1-3.
- **5_** Non vocal sounds. Thumps Bangs, Pops, Footsteps, etc.

Source Grading: 5

- **M_** Multiple voices heard, unable to differentiate.
- **U_** The gender or age cannot be determined.
- **W_** The voice is clearly that of a child.
- **X_** The voice is clearly that of a woman.
- **Y_** The voice is clearly that of a man.
- **Z_** The recording is of an animal sound (Barking, Meowing, Vocalizations only)

- Note that many EVPs may contain portions falling into multiple categories. Parts may be clear then fade out. Vocalizations may be preceded or followed by non-vocal sounds. Thus a particular EVP may have multiple classifications. If you are classifying the overall EVP, use the most predominate characteristics.

To Grade your EVP, select the appropriate **letter** from the first column, **number** from the second column and finally **letter** from the third. Enter that grading under the "Classification" on the Post Investigation Summary Sheet.

Post Investigation Summary Sheet 6__

Time : _____ Classification: _____ Processing Applied? No
____ Yes ____ (Type) _____

Transcript :
_____
_____

Any external stimuli applied? No ____ Yes ____ (Type)
_____
_____

Leading Questions or Conversation
_____
_____

Any other sounds recorded?
_____Reviewed
By: _____, _____

Time : _____ Classification: _____ Processing Applied? No
___ Yes ___ (Type) _____

Transcript :
_____
_____

Any external stimuli applied? No _____ Yes _____ (Type)
_____
_____

Leading Questions or Conversation
_____
_____

Any other sounds recorded?
_____Reviewed
By: _____, _____

Time : _____ Classification: _____ Processing Applied? No
___ Yes ___ (Type) _____

Transcript :
_____
_____

Any external stimuli applied? No _____ Yes _____ (Type)
_____
_____

Leading Questions or Conversation
_____
_____

Any other sounds recorded?
_____Reviewed
By: _____, _____

1

REPORTING INVESTIGATOR NAME OR NUMBER:_____

~ EVP Log Book ~

URN: _____ , _____ , _____ - _____ - _____

Day Month Year Number Type

Location :

_____

Investigating Team : _____

_____

_____

_____

_____

Set Up Sheet - Hardware Configuration

Audio Equipment ----- _____

_____

_____

_____

Support Equipment -- _____

_____

_____

Sources of Interaction - _____

_____

_____

Audio Equipment ----- _____

_____

_____

_____

Support Equipment -- _____

_____

_____

_____

Sources of Interaction - _____

_____

_____

_____

3____

Layout of Target Area - (Sketch Below)

Real Time Event Log 4___
Line Time Event Witnessed

_____ - _____ -
_____
_____ - _____

_____ - _____ -
_____
_____ - _____

_____ - _____ -
_____
_____ - _____

_____ - _____ -
_____
_____ - _____

_____ - _____ -
_____
_____ - _____

_____ - _____ -
_____
_____ - _____

_____ - _____ -
_____
_____ - _____

_____ - _____ -
_____
_____ - _____

Quality Grading: (EVP Research Standards)

- **A_** Heard and understood clearly without any signal processing at all, Like a normal voice.
- **B_** Processed using analog filtering, but most who hear it can decipher the content. There is little disagreement on what is recorded.
- **C_** Processed using analog filtering, but still hard to hear. Potential for disagreement on content.
- **D_** Digital processing employed to make out anything at all. Disagreement over content, some may not hear anything.
- **E_** Most hear nothing; some may claim to hear a voice. Processing may result in different messages being heard.

Content Grading

- **1_** Easily related to surroundings. For instance: A soldier who was killed mentioning the battle, etc.
- **2_** Unrelated but meaningful, such as a statement "I love you". Could be for anyone or maybe no one present.
- **3_** Gibberish. Meaningless groups of words but still recognizable as words or phrases.
- **4_** Utterances. Vocalized sounds not words. Includes grunts and groans. Before classifying here make sure you are not dealing with a foreign language which should actually be in categories 1-3.
- **5_** Non vocal sounds. Thumps Bangs, Pops, Footsteps, etc.

Source Grading: 5

- **M_** Multiple voices heard, unable to differentiate.
- **U_** The gender or age cannot be determined.
- **W_** The voice is clearly that of a child.
- **X_** The voice is clearly that of a woman.
- **Y_** The voice is clearly that of a man.
- **Z_** The recording is of an animal sound (Barking, Meowing, Vocalizations only)

- Note that many EVPs may contain portions falling into multiple categories. Parts may be clear then fade out. Vocalizations may be preceded or followed by non-vocal sounds. Thus a particular EVP may have multiple classifications. If you are classifying the overall EVP, use the most predominate characteristics.

To Grade your EVP, select the appropriate **letter** from the first column, **number** from the second column and finally **letter** from the third. Enter that grading under the "Classification" on the Post Investigation Summary Sheet.

Post Investigation Summary Sheet 6__

Time : _____ Classification: _____ Processing Applied? No ___ Yes ___ (Type) _____

Transcript :

_____
_____

Any external stimuli applied? No _____ Yes _____ (Type)

_____
_____

Leading Questions or Conversation

_____
_____

Any other sounds recorded?

_____Reviewed
By: _____, _____

Time : _____ **Classification:** _____ **Processing Applied? No** ___ **Yes** ___ **(Type)** _____

Transcript :
_____
_____

Any external stimuli applied? No _____ **Yes** _____ **(Type)**
_____
_____

Leading Questions or Conversation
_____
_____

Any other sounds recorded?
_____**Reviewed By:** _____ , _____

Time : _____ **Classification:** _____ **Processing Applied? No** ___ **Yes** ___ **(Type)** _____

Transcript :
_____
_____

Any external stimuli applied? No _____ **Yes** _____ **(Type)**
_____
_____

Leading Questions or Conversation
_____
_____

Any other sounds recorded?
_____**Reviewed By:** _____ , _____

REPORTING INVESTIGATOR NAME OR
NUMBER:_____

~ EVP Log Book ~

URN: _____ , _____ , _____ - _____ ˙˙ _____

Day Month Year Number Type

Location :

_____

Investigating Team : _____

_____

_____

_____

_____

Set Up Sheet - Hardware Configuration

Audio Equipment ----- _____

_____

_____

_____

_____

Support Equipment -- _____

_____

_____

Sources of Interaction - _____

_____

_____

Audio Equipment ----- _____

_____

_____

_____

Support Equipment -- _____

_____

_____

_____

Sources of Interaction - _____

_____

_____

_____

3___

Layout of Target Area - (Sketch Below)

Real Time Event Log 4___
Line Time Event Witnessed

_____ - _____ - ____

_____

_____ - _____

_____ - _____ - ____

_____

_____ - _____

_____ - _____ - ____

_____

_____ - _____

_____ - _____ - ____

_____

_____ - _____

_____ - _____ - ____

_____

_____ - _____

_____ - _____ - ____

_____

_____ - _____

_____ - _____ - ____

_____

_____ - _____

_____ - _____ - ____

_____

_____ - _____

Quality Grading: (EVP Research Standards)

- **A_** Heard and understood clearly without any signal processing at all, Like a normal voice.
- **B_** Processed using analog filtering, but most who hear it can decipher the content. There is little disagreement on what is recorded.
- **C_** Processed using analog filtering, but still hard to hear. Potential for disagreement on content.
- **D_** Digital processing employed to make out anything at all. Disagreement over content, some may not hear anything.
- **E_** Most hear nothing; some may claim to hear a voice. Processing may result in different messages being heard.

Content Grading

- **1_** Easily related to surroundings. For instance: A soldier who was killed mentioning the battle, etc.
- **2_** Unrelated but meaningful, such as a statement "I love you". Could be for anyone or maybe no one present.
- **3_** Gibberish. Meaningless groups of words but still recognizable as words or phrases.
- **4_** Utterances. Vocalized sounds not words. Includes grunts and groans. Before classifying here make sure you are not dealing with a foreign language which should actually be in categories 1-3.
- **5_** Non vocal sounds. Thumps Bangs, Pops, Footsteps, etc.

Source Grading: 5

- **M_** Multiple voices heard, unable to differentiate.
- **U_** The gender or age cannot be determined.
- **W_** The voice is clearly that of a child.
- **X_** The voice is clearly that of a woman.
- **Y_** The voice is clearly that of a man.
- **Z_** The recording is of an animal sound (Barking, Meowing, Vocalizations only)

- Note that many EVPs may contain portions falling into multiple categories. Parts may be clear then fade out. Vocalizations may be preceded or followed by non-vocal sounds. Thus a particular EVP may have multiple classifications. If you are classifying the overall EVP, use the most predominate characteristics.

To Grade your EVP, select the appropriate **letter** from the first column, **number** from the second column and finally **letter** from the third. Enter that grading under the "Classification" on the Post Investigation Summary Sheet.

Post Investigation Summary Sheet 6__

Time : _____ Classification: _____ Processing Applied? No ____ Yes ____ (Type) _____

Transcript :

_____
_____

Any external stimuli applied? No _____ Yes _____ (Type)

_____
_____

Leading Questions or Conversation

_____
_____

Any other sounds recorded?

_____Reviewed
By: _____, _____

Time : _____ Classification: _____ Processing Applied? No
___ Yes ___ (Type) _____

Transcript :
_____
_____

Any external stimuli applied? No ____ Yes ____ (Type)
_____
_____

Leading Questions or Conversation
_____
_____

Any other sounds recorded?
_____Reviewed
By: _____, _____

Time : _____ Classification: _____ Processing Applied? No
___ Yes ___ (Type) _____

Transcript :
_____
_____

Any external stimuli applied? No ____ Yes ____ (Type)
_____
_____

Leading Questions or Conversation
_____
_____

Any other sounds recorded?
_____Reviewed
By: _____, _____

1

REPORTING INVESTIGATOR NAME OR
NUMBER:_____

~ EVP Log Book ~

URN: _____ , _____ , _____ - _____ - _____

Day Month Year Number Type

Location :
_____

Investigating Team : _____

_____

_____

_____

_____

Set Up Sheet - Hardware Configuration

Audio Equipment ----- _____

_____

_____

_____

_____

Support Equipment -- _____

_____

_____

Sources of Interaction - _____

_____

_____

Audio Equipment ----- _____

_____

_____

_____

Support Equipment -- _____

_____

_____

_____

Sources of Interaction - _____

_____

_____

_____

3___

Layout of Target Area - (Sketch Below)

Real Time Event Log 4___
Line Time Event Witnessed

_____ - _____ -

_____

_____ - _____

_____ - _____ -

_____

_____ - _____

_____ - _____ -

_____

_____ - _____

_____ - _____ -

_____

_____ - _____

_____ - _____ -

_____

_____ - _____

_____ - _____ -

_____

_____ - _____

_____ - _____ -

_____

_____ - _____

Quality Grading: (EVP Research Standards)

- **A_** Heard and understood clearly without any signal processing at all, Like a normal voice.
- **B_** Processed using analog filtering, but most who hear it can decipher the content. There is little disagreement on what is recorded.
- **C_** Processed using analog filtering, but still hard to hear. Potential for disagreement on content.
- **D_** Digital processing employed to make out anything at all. Disagreement over content, some may not hear anything.
- **E_** Most hear nothing; some may claim to hear a voice. Processing may result in different messages being heard.

Content Grading

- **1_** Easily related to surroundings. For instance: A soldier who was killed mentioning the battle, etc.
- **2_** Unrelated but meaningful, such as a statement "I love you". Could be for anyone or maybe no one present.
- **3_** Gibberish. Meaningless groups of words but still recognizable as words or phrases.
- **4_** Utterances. Vocalized sounds not words. Includes grunts and groans. Before classifying here make sure you are not dealing with a foreign language which should actually be in categories 1-3.
- **5_** Non vocal sounds. Thumps Bangs, Pops, Footsteps, etc.

Source Grading: 5

- **M_** Multiple voices heard, unable to differentiate.
- **U_** The gender or age cannot be determined.
- **W_** The voice is clearly that of a child.
- **X_** The voice is clearly that of a woman.
- **Y_** The voice is clearly that of a man.
- **Z_** The recording is of an animal sound (Barking, Meowing, Vocalizations only)

- Note that many EVPs may contain portions falling into multiple categories. Parts may be clear then fade out. Vocalizations may be preceded or followed by non-vocal sounds. Thus a particular EVP may have multiple classifications. If you are classifying the overall EVP, use the most predominate characteristics.

To Grade your EVP, select the appropriate **letter** from the first column, **number** from the second column and finally **letter** from the third. Enter that grading under the "Classification" on the Post Investigation Summary Sheet.

Post Investigation Summary Sheet 6__

Time : _____ Classification: _____ Processing Applied? No ___ Yes ___ (Type) _____

Transcript :

_____

_____

Any external stimuli applied? No ____ Yes ____ (Type)

_____

_____

Leading Questions or Conversation

_____

_____

Any other sounds recorded?

_____Reviewed

By: _____, _____

Time : _____ Classification: _____ Processing Applied? No ___ Yes ___ (Type) _____

Transcript :

_____
_____

Any external stimuli applied? No ____ Yes ____ (Type)

_____
_____

Leading Questions or Conversation

_____
_____

Any other sounds recorded?

_____Reviewed
By: _____, _____

Time : _____ Classification: _____ Processing Applied? No ___ Yes ___ (Type) _____

Transcript :

_____
_____

Any external stimuli applied? No ____ Yes ____ (Type)

_____
_____

Leading Questions or Conversation

_____
_____

Any other sounds recorded?

_____Reviewed
By: _____, _____

**REPORTING INVESTIGATOR NAME OR
NUMBER:**_____

~ EVP Log Book ~

URN: _____ , _____ , _____ - _____ - _____

Day Month Year Number Type

Location :

_____

Investigating Team : _____

_____

_____

_____

_____

Set Up Sheet - Hardware Configuration

Audio Equipment ----- _____

_____

_____

_____

_____

Support Equipment -- _____

_____

_____

Sources of Interaction - _____

_____

_____

Audio Equipment ----- _____

_____

_____

_____

Support Equipment -- _____

_____

_____

_____

Sources of Interaction - _____

_____

_____

_____

3___

Layout of Target Area - (Sketch Below)

Real Time Event Log 4___
Line Time Event Witnessed

_____ - _____ - ____

_____

_____ - _____

_____ - _____ - ____

_____

_____ - _____

_____ - _____ - ____

_____

_____ - _____

_____ - _____ - ____

_____

_____ - _____

_____ - _____ - ____

_____

_____ - _____

_____ - _____ - ____

_____

_____ - _____

_____ - _____ - ____

_____

_____ - _____

_____ - _____ - ____

_____

_____ - _____

_____ - _____ - ____

_____

_____ - _____

Quality Grading: (EVP Research Standards)

- **A_** Heard and understood clearly without any signal processing at all, Like a normal voice.
- **B_** Processed using analog filtering, but most who hear it can decipher the content. There is little disagreement on what is recorded.
- **C_** Processed using analog filtering, but still hard to hear. Potential for disagreement on content.
- **D_** Digital processing employed to make out anything at all. Disagreement over content, some may not hear anything.
- **E_** Most hear nothing; some may claim to hear a voice. Processing may result in different messages being heard.

Content Grading

- **1_** Easily related to surroundings. For instance: A soldier who was killed mentioning the battle, etc.
- **2_** Unrelated but meaningful, such as a statement "I love you". Could be for anyone or maybe no one present.
- **3_** Gibberish. Meaningless groups of words but still recognizable as words or phrases.
- **4_** Utterances. Vocalized sounds not words. Includes grunts and groans. Before classifying here make sure you are not dealing with a foreign language which should actually be in categories 1-3.
- **5_** Non vocal sounds. Thumps Bangs, Pops, Footsteps, etc.

Source Grading: 5

- **M_** Multiple voices heard, unable to differentiate.
- **U_** The gender or age cannot be determined.
- **W_** The voice is clearly that of a child.
- **X_** The voice is clearly that of a woman.
- **Y_** The voice is clearly that of a man.
- **Z_** The recording is of an animal sound (Barking, Meowing, Vocalizations only)

- Note that many EVPs may contain portions falling into multiple categories. Parts may be clear then fade out. Vocalizations may be preceded or followed by non-vocal sounds. Thus a particular EVP may have multiple classifications. If you are classifying the overall EVP, use the most predominate characteristics.

To Grade your EVP, select the appropriate **letter** from the first column, **number** from the second column and finally **letter** from the third. Enter that grading under the "Classification" on the Post Investigation Summary Sheet.

Post Investigation Summary Sheet 6___

Time : _____ Classification: _____ **Processing Applied? No**
___ Yes ___ (Type) _____

Transcript :
_____
_____

Any external stimuli applied? No _____ Yes _____ (Type)
_____
_____

Leading Questions or Conversation
_____
_____

Any other sounds recorded?
_____**Reviewed**
By: _____, _____

Time : _____ Classification: _____ Processing Applied? No
___ Yes ___ (Type) _____

Transcript :

_____
_____

Any external stimuli applied? No _____ Yes _____ (Type)

_____
_____

Leading Questions or Conversation

_____
_____

Any other sounds recorded?

_____Reviewed
By: _____, _____

Time : _____ Classification: _____ Processing Applied? No
___ Yes ___ (Type) _____

Transcript :

_____
_____

Any external stimuli applied? No _____ Yes _____ (Type)

_____
_____

Leading Questions or Conversation

_____
_____

Any other sounds recorded?

_____Reviewed
By: _____, _____

**REPORTING INVESTIGATOR NAME OR
NUMBER:**_____

~ EVP Log Book ~

URN: _____ , _____ , _____ - _____ - _____

Day Month Year Number Type

Location :

_____

Investigating Team : _____

_____

_____

_____

_____

Set Up Sheet - Hardware Configuration

Audio Equipment ----- _____

_____

_____

_____

_____

Support Equipment -- _____

_____

_____

Sources of Interaction - _____

_____

_____

Audio Equipment ----- _____

_____

_____

_____

Support Equipment -- _____

_____

_____

_____

Sources of Interaction - _____

_____

_____

_____

3___

Layout of Target Area - (Sketch Below)

Real Time Event Log 4___
Line Time Event Witnessed

_____ - _____ -

_____

_____ - _____

_____ - _____ -

_____

_____ - _____

_____ - _____ -

_____

_____ - _____

_____ - _____ -

_____

_____ - _____

_____ - _____ -

_____

_____ - _____

_____ - _____ -

_____

_____ - _____

Quality Grading: (EVP Research Standards)

- **A_** Heard and understood clearly without any signal processing at all, Like a normal voice.
- **B_** Processed using analog filtering, but most who hear it can decipher the content. There is little disagreement on what is recorded.
- **C_** Processed using analog filtering, but still hard to hear. Potential for disagreement on content.
- **D_** Digital processing employed to make out anything at all. Disagreement over content, some may not hear anything.
- **E_** Most hear nothing; some may claim to hear a voice. Processing may result in different messages being heard.

Content Grading

- **1_** Easily related to surroundings. For instance: A soldier who was killed mentioning the battle, etc.
- **2_** Unrelated but meaningful, such as a statement "I love you". Could be for anyone or maybe no one present.
- **3_** Gibberish. Meaningless groups of words but still recognizable as words or phrases.
- **4_** Utterances. Vocalized sounds not words. Includes grunts and groans. Before classifying here make sure you are not dealing with a foreign language which should actually be in categories 1-3.
- **5_** Non vocal sounds. Thumps Bangs, Pops, Footsteps, etc.

Source Grading: 5

- **M_** Multiple voices heard, unable to differentiate.
- **U_** The gender or age cannot be determined.
- **W_** The voice is clearly that of a child.
- **X_** The voice is clearly that of a woman.
- **Y_** The voice is clearly that of a man.
- **Z_** The recording is of an animal sound (Barking, Meowing, Vocalizations only)

- Note that many EVPs may contain portions falling into multiple categories. Parts may be clear then fade out. Vocalizations may be preceded or followed by non-vocal sounds. Thus a particular EVP may have multiple classifications. If you are classifying the overall EVP, use the most predominate characteristics.

To Grade your EVP, select the appropriate **letter** from the first column, **number** from the second column and finally **letter** from the third. Enter that grading under the "Classification" on the Post Investigation Summary Sheet.

Post Investigation Summary Sheet 6__

Time : _____ Classification: _____ Processing Applied? No ____ Yes ___ (Type) _____-

Transcript :

_____

_____

Any external stimuli applied? No _____ Yes _____ (Type)

_____

_____

Leading Questions or Conversation

_____

_____

Any other sounds recorded?

_____Reviewed

By: _____, _____

Time : _____ Classification: _____ Processing Applied? No ___ Yes ___ (Type) _____

Transcript :

_____

_____

Any external stimuli applied? No ____ Yes ____ (Type)

_____

_____

Leading Questions or Conversation

_____

_____

Any other sounds recorded?

_____**Reviewed By:** _____, _____

Time : _____ Classification: _____ Processing Applied? No ___ Yes ___ (Type) _____

Transcript :

_____

_____

Any external stimuli applied? No ____ Yes ____ (Type)

_____

_____

Leading Questions or Conversation

_____

_____

Any other sounds recorded?

_____**Reviewed By:** _____, _____

1

REPORTING INVESTIGATOR NAME OR NUMBER:_____

~ EVP Log Book ~

URN: _____ , _____ , _____ - _____ - _____

Day Month Year Number Type

Location :

_____

Investigating Team : _____

_____

_____

_____

_____

Set Up Sheet - Hardware Configuration

Audio Equipment ----- _____

_____

_____

_____

Support Equipment -- _____

_____

Sources of Interaction - _____

_____

_____

Audio Equipment ----- _____

_____

_____

_____

Support Equipment -- _____

_____

_____

_____

Sources of Interaction - _____

_____

_____

_____

3___

Layout of Target Area - (Sketch Below)

Real Time Event Log 4___
Line Time Event Witnessed

_____ - _____ - _____

_____

_____ - _____

_____ - _____ - _____

_____

_____ - _____

_____ - _____ - _____

_____

_____ - _____

_____ - _____ - _____

_____

_____ - _____

_____ - _____ - _____

_____

_____ - _____

_____ - _____ - _____

_____

_____ - _____

_____ - _____ - _____

_____

_____ - _____

Quality Grading: (EVP Research Standards)

- **A_** Heard and understood clearly without any signal processing at all, Like a normal voice.
- **B_** Processed using analog filtering, but most who hear it can decipher the content. There is little disagreement on what is recorded.
- **C_** Processed using analog filtering, but still hard to hear. Potential for disagreement on content.
- **D_** Digital processing employed to make out anything at all. Disagreement over content, some may not hear anything.
- **E_** Most hear nothing; some may claim to hear a voice. Processing may result in different messages being heard.

Content Grading

- **1_** Easily related to surroundings. For instance: A soldier who was killed mentioning the battle, etc.
- **2_** Unrelated but meaningful, such as a statement "I love you". Could be for anyone or maybe no one present.
- **3_** Gibberish. Meaningless groups of words but still recognizable as words or phrases.
- **4_** Utterances. Vocalized sounds not words. Includes grunts and groans. Before classifying here make sure you are not dealing with a foreign language which should actually be in categories 1-3.
- **5_** Non vocal sounds. Thumps Bangs, Pops, Footsteps, etc.

Source Grading: 5

- **M_** Multiple voices heard, unable to differentiate.
- **U_** The gender or age cannot be determined.
- **W_** The voice is clearly that of a child.
- **X_** The voice is clearly that of a woman.
- **Y_** The voice is clearly that of a man.
- **Z_** The recording is of an animal sound (Barking, Meowing, Vocalizations only)

- Note that many EVPs may contain portions falling into multiple categories. Parts may be clear then fade out. Vocalizations may be preceded or followed by non-vocal sounds. Thus a particular EVP may have multiple classifications. If you are classifying the overall EVP, use the most predominate characteristics.

To Grade your EVP, select the appropriate **letter** from the first column, **number** from the second column and finally **letter** from the third. Enter that grading under the "Classification" on the Post Investigation Summary Sheet.

Post Investigation Summary Sheet 6__

Time : _____ Classification: _____ Processing Applied? No ___ Yes ___ (Type) _____

Transcript :
_____
_____

Any external stimuli applied? No ____ Yes ____ (Type)
_____
_____

Leading Questions or Conversation
_____
_____

Any other sounds recorded?
_____Reviewed
By: _____, _____

Time : _____ Classification: _____ Processing Applied? No
___ Yes ___ (Type) _____

Transcript :
_____
_____

Any external stimuli applied? No _____ Yes _____ (Type)
_____
_____

Leading Questions or Conversation
_____
_____

Any other sounds recorded?
_____Reviewed
By: _____, _____

Time : _____ Classification: _____ Processing Applied? No
___ Yes ___ (Type) _____

Transcript :
_____
_____

Any external stimuli applied? No _____ Yes _____ (Type)
_____
_____

Leading Questions or Conversation
_____
_____

Any other sounds recorded?
_____Reviewed
By: _____, _____

1

REPORTING INVESTIGATOR NAME OR
NUMBER:_____

~ EVP Log Book ~

URN: _____ , _____ , _____ - _____ - _____

Day Month Year Number Type

Location :

_____

Investigating Team : _____

_____

_____

_____

_____

Set Up Sheet - Hardware Configuration

Audio Equipment ----- _____

_____

_____

_____

_____

Support Equipment -- _____

_____

_____

Sources of Interaction - _____

_____

_____

Audio Equipment ----- _____

_____

_____

_____

Support Equipment -- _____

_____

_____

_____

Sources of Interaction - _____

_____

_____

_____

3___

Layout of Target Area - (Sketch Below)

Real Time Event Log 4___
Line Time Event Witnessed

_____ - _____ -
_____
_____ - _____
_____ - _____ -
_____
_____ - _____
_____ - _____ -
_____
_____ - _____
_____ - _____ -
_____
_____ - _____
_____ - _____ -
_____
_____ - _____
_____ - _____ -
_____
_____ - _____
_____ - _____ -
_____
_____ - _____
_____ - _____ -
_____
_____ - _____

Quality Grading: (EVP Research Standards)

- o **A_** Heard and understood clearly without any signal processing at all, Like a normal voice.
- o **B_** Processed using analog filtering, but most who hear it can decipher the content. There is little disagreement on what is recorded.
- o **C_** Processed using analog filtering, but still hard to hear. Potential for disagreement on content.
- o **D_** Digital processing employed to make out anything at all. Disagreement over content, some may not hear anything.
- o **E_** Most hear nothing; some may claim to hear a voice. Processing may result in different messages being heard.

Content Grading

- o **1_** Easily related to surroundings. For instance: A soldier who was killed mentioning the battle, etc.
- o **2_** Unrelated but meaningful, such as a statement "I love you". Could be for anyone or maybe no one present.
- o **3_** Gibberish. Meaningless groups of words but still recognizable as words or phrases.
- o **4_** Utterances. Vocalized sounds not words. Includes grunts and groans. Before classifying here make sure you are not dealing with a foreign language which should actually be in categories 1-3.
- o **5_** Non vocal sounds. Thumps Bangs, Pops, Footsteps, etc.

Source Grading: 5

- o **M_** Multiple voices heard, unable to differentiate.
- o **U_** The gender or age cannot be determined.
- o **W_** The voice is clearly that of a child.
- o **X_** The voice is clearly that of a woman.
- o **Y_** The voice is clearly that of a man.
- o **Z_** The recording is of an animal sound (Barking, Meowing, Vocalizations only)

- Note that many EVPs may contain portions falling into multiple categories. Parts may be clear then fade out. Vocalizations may be preceded or followed by non-vocal sounds. Thus a particular EVP may have multiple classifications. If you are classifying the overall EVP, use the most predominate characteristics.

To Grade your EVP, select the appropriate **letter** from the first column, **number** from the second column and finally **letter** from the third. Enter that grading under the "Classification" on the Post Investigation Summary Sheet.

Post Investigation Summary Sheet 6__

Time : _____ Classification: _____ Processing Applied? No ___ Yes ___ (Type) _____

Transcript :
_____
_____

Any external stimuli applied? No ____ Yes ____ (Type)
_____
_____

Leading Questions or Conversation
_____
_____

Any other sounds recorded?
_____Reviewed
By: _____, _____

Time : _____ Classification: _____ Processing Applied? No
___ Yes ___ (Type) _____

Transcript :
_____
_____

Any external stimuli applied? No ____ Yes ____ (Type)
_____
_____

Leading Questions or Conversation
_____
_____

Any other sounds recorded?
_____Reviewed
By: _____, _____

Time : _____ Classification: _____ Processing Applied? No
___ Yes ___ (Type) _____

Transcript :
_____
_____

Any external stimuli applied? No ____ Yes ____ (Type)
_____
_____

Leading Questions or Conversation
_____
_____

Any other sounds recorded?
_____Reviewed
By: _____, _____

REPORTING INVESTIGATOR NAME OR NUMBER:_____

~ EVP Log Book ~

URN: _____ , _____ , _____ - _____ - _____

Day Month Year Number Type

Location :

_____

Investigating Team : _____

_____

_____

_____

_____

Set Up Sheet - Hardware Configuration

Audio Equipment ----- _____

_____

_____

_____

_____

Support Equipment -- _____

_____

_____

Sources of Interaction - _____

_____

_____

Audio Equipment ----- _____

_____

_____

_____

Support Equipment -- _____

_____

_____

_____

Sources of Interaction - _____

_____

_____

_____

3___

Layout of Target Area - (Sketch Below)

Real Time Event Log 4___
Line Time Event Witnessed

_____ - _____ -
_____
_____ - _____

_____ - _____ -
_____
_____ - _____

_____ - _____ -
_____
_____ - _____

_____ - _____ -
_____
_____ - _____

_____ - _____ -
_____
_____ - _____

_____ - _____ -
_____
_____ - _____

_____ - _____ -
_____
_____ - _____

_____ - _____ -
_____
_____ - _____

Quality Grading: (EVP Research Standards)

- **A_** Heard and understood clearly without any signal processing at all, Like a normal voice.
- **B_** Processed using analog filtering, but most who hear it can decipher the content. There is little disagreement on what is recorded.
- **C_** Processed using analog filtering, but still hard to hear. Potential for disagreement on content.
- **D_** Digital processing employed to make out anything at all. Disagreement over content, some may not hear anything.
- **E_** Most hear nothing; some may claim to hear a voice. Processing may result in different messages being heard.

Content Grading

- **1_** Easily related to surroundings. For instance: A soldier who was killed mentioning the battle, etc.
- **2_** Unrelated but meaningful, such as a statement "I love you". Could be for anyone or maybe no one present.
- **3_** Gibberish. Meaningless groups of words but still recognizable as words or phrases.
- **4_** Utterances. Vocalized sounds not words. Includes grunts and groans. Before classifying here make sure you are not dealing with a foreign language which should actually be in categories 1-3.
- **5_** Non vocal sounds. Thumps Bangs, Pops, Footsteps, etc.

Source Grading: 5

- **M_** Multiple voices heard, unable to differentiate.
- **U_** The gender or age cannot be determined.
- **W_** The voice is clearly that of a child.
- **X_** The voice is clearly that of a woman.
- **Y_** The voice is clearly that of a man.
- **Z_** The recording is of an animal sound (Barking, Meowing, Vocalizations only)

- Note that many EVPs may contain portions falling into multiple categories. Parts may be clear then fade out. Vocalizations may be preceded or followed by non-vocal sounds. Thus a particular EVP may have multiple classifications. If you are classifying the overall EVP, use the most predominate characteristics.

To Grade your EVP, select the appropriate **letter** from the first column, **number** from the second column and finally **letter** from the third. Enter that grading under the "Classification" on the Post Investigation Summary Sheet.

Post Investigation Summary Sheet 6__

Time : _____ Classification: _____ Processing Applied? No ____ Yes ____ (Type) _____

Transcript :

_____
_____

Any external stimuli applied? No ____ Yes ____ (Type)

_____
_____

Leading Questions or Conversation

_____
_____

Any other sounds recorded?

_____Reviewed
By: _____, _____

Time : _____ Classification: _____ Processing Applied? No
___ Yes ___ (Type) _____

Transcript :
_____
_____

Any external stimuli applied? No ____ Yes ____ (Type)
_____
_____

Leading Questions or Conversation
_____
_____

Any other sounds recorded?
_____Reviewed
By: _____, _____

Time : _____ Classification: _____ Processing Applied? No
___ Yes ___ (Type) _____

Transcript :
_____
_____

Any external stimuli applied? No ____ Yes ____ (Type)
_____
_____

Leading Questions or Conversation
_____
_____

Any other sounds recorded?
_____Reviewed
By: _____, _____

1

**REPORTING INVESTIGATOR NAME OR
NUMBER:**_____

~ EVP Log Book ~

URN: _____ , _____ , _____ - _____ - _____

Day Month Year Number Type

Location :
_____

Investigating Team : _____

_____

_____

_____

_____

Set Up Sheet - Hardware Configuration

Audio Equipment ----- _____

_____

_____

_____

Support Equipment -- _____

_____

_____

Sources of Interaction - _____

_____

_____

Audio Equipment ----- _____

_____

_____

_____

Support Equipment -- _____

_____

_____

_____

Sources of Interaction - _____

_____

_____

_____

3___

Layout of Target Area - (Sketch Below)

Real Time Event Log 4___
Line Time Event Witnessed

_____ - _____ -

_____

_____ - _____

_____ - _____ -

_____ - _____

_____ - _____ -

_____ - _____

_____ - _____ -

_____ - _____

_____ - _____ -

_____ - _____

_____ - _____ -

_____ - _____

_____ - _____ -

_____ - _____

_____ - _____ -

_____ - _____

Quality Grading: (EVP Research Standards)

- **A_** Heard and understood clearly without any signal processing at all, Like a normal voice.
- **B_** Processed using analog filtering, but most who hear it can decipher the content. There is little disagreement on what is recorded.
- **C_** Processed using analog filtering, but still hard to hear. Potential for disagreement on content.
- **D_** Digital processing employed to make out anything at all. Disagreement over content, some may not hear anything.
- **E_** Most hear nothing; some may claim to hear a voice. Processing may result in different messages being heard.

Content Grading

- **1_** Easily related to surroundings. For instance: A soldier who was killed mentioning the battle, etc.
- **2_** Unrelated but meaningful, such as a statement "I love you". Could be for anyone or maybe no one present.
- **3_** Gibberish. Meaningless groups of words but still recognizable as words or phrases.
- **4_** Utterances. Vocalized sounds not words. Includes grunts and groans. Before classifying here make sure you are not dealing with a foreign language which should actually be in categories 1-3.
- **5_** Non vocal sounds. Thumps Bangs, Pops, Footsteps, etc.

Source Grading: 5

- **M_** Multiple voices heard, unable to differentiate.
- **U_** The gender or age cannot be determined.
- **W_** The voice is clearly that of a child.
- **X_** The voice is clearly that of a woman.
- **Y_** The voice is clearly that of a man.
- **Z_** The recording is of an animal sound (Barking, Meowing, Vocalizations only)

- Note that many EVPs may contain portions falling into multiple categories. Parts may be clear then fade out. Vocalizations may be preceded or followed by non-vocal sounds. Thus a particular EVP may have multiple classifications. If you are classifying the overall EVP, use the most predominate characteristics.

To Grade your EVP, select the appropriate **letter** from the first column, **number** from the second column and finally **letter** from the third. Enter that grading under the "Classification" on the Post Investigation Summary Sheet.

Post Investigation Summary Sheet 6__

Time : _____ Classification: _____ Processing Applied? No ___ Yes ___ (Type) _____

Transcript :
_____
_____

Any external stimuli applied? No _____ Yes _____ (Type)
_____
_____

Leading Questions or Conversation
_____
_____

Any other sounds recorded?
_____Reviewed
By: _____, _____

Time : _____ Classification: _____ Processing Applied? No
___ Yes ___ (Type) _____

Transcript :
_____
_____

Any external stimuli applied? No ____ Yes ____ (Type)
_____
_____

Leading Questions or Conversation
_____
_____

Any other sounds recorded?
_____Reviewed
By: _____, _____

Time : _____ Classification: _____ Processing Applied? No
___ Yes ___ (Type) _____

Transcript :
_____
_____

Any external stimuli applied? No ____ Yes ____ (Type)
_____
_____

Leading Questions or Conversation
_____
_____

Any other sounds recorded?
_____Reviewed
By: _____, _____

REPORTING INVESTIGATOR NAME OR
NUMBER:_____

~ EVP Log Book ~

URN: _____ , _____ , _____ - _____ - _____

Day Month Year Number Type

Location :

_____

Investigating Team : _____

_____

_____

_____

_____

Set Up Sheet - Hardware Configuration

Audio Equipment ----- _____

_____

_____

_____

_____

Support Equipment -- _____

_____

_____

Sources of Interaction - _____

_____

_____

Audio Equipment ----- _____

_____

_____

_____

Support Equipment -- _____

_____

_____

_____

Sources of Interaction - _____

_____

_____

_____

3___

Layout of Target Area - (Sketch Below)

Real Time Event Log 4___
Line Time Event Witnessed

_____ - _____ - _____

_____

_____ - _____

_____ - _____ - _____

_____

_____ - _____

_____ - _____ - _____

_____

_____ - _____

_____ - _____ - _____

_____

_____ - _____

_____ - _____ - _____

_____

_____ - _____

_____ - _____ - _____

_____

_____ - _____

_____ - _____ - _____

_____

_____ - _____

Quality Grading: (EVP Research Standards)

- **A_** Heard and understood clearly without any signal processing at all, Like a normal voice.
- **B_** Processed using analog filtering, but most who hear it can decipher the content. There is little disagreement on what is recorded.
- **C_** Processed using analog filtering, but still hard to hear. Potential for disagreement on content.
- **D_** Digital processing employed to make out anything at all. Disagreement over content, some may not hear anything.
- **E_** Most hear nothing; some may claim to hear a voice. Processing may result in different messages being heard.

Content Grading

- **1_** Easily related to surroundings. For instance: A soldier who was killed mentioning the battle, etc.
- **2_** Unrelated but meaningful, such as a statement "I love you". Could be for anyone or maybe no one present.
- **3_** Gibberish. Meaningless groups of words but still recognizable as words or phrases.
- **4_** Utterances. Vocalized sounds not words. Includes grunts and groans. Before classifying here make sure you are not dealing with a foreign language which should actually be in categories 1-3.
- **5_** Non vocal sounds. Thumps Bangs, Pops, Footsteps, etc.

Source Grading: 5

- **M_** Multiple voices heard, unable to differentiate.
- **U_** The gender or age cannot be determined.
- **W_** The voice is clearly that of a child.
- **X_** The voice is clearly that of a woman.
- **Y_** The voice is clearly that of a man.
- **Z_** The recording is of an animal sound (Barking, Meowing, Vocalizations only)

- Note that many EVPs may contain portions falling into multiple categories. Parts may be clear then fade out. Vocalizations may be preceded or followed by non-vocal sounds. Thus a particular EVP may have multiple classifications. If you are classifying the overall EVP, use the most predominate characteristics.

To Grade your EVP, select the appropriate **letter** from the first column, **number** from the second column and finally **letter** from the third. Enter that grading under the "Classification" on the Post Investigation Summary Sheet.

Post Investigation Summary Sheet 6__

Time : _____ Classification: _____ Processing Applied? No ___ Yes ___ (Type) _____

Transcript :

_____

_____

Any external stimuli applied? No _____ **Yes** _____ **(Type)**

_____

_____

Leading Questions or Conversation

_____

_____

Any other sounds recorded?

_____Reviewed

By: _____, _____

Time : _____ Classification: _____ Processing Applied? No ___ Yes ___ (Type) _____

Transcript :

_____

_____

Any external stimuli applied? No ____ Yes ____ (Type)

_____

_____

Leading Questions or Conversation

_____

_____

Any other sounds recorded?

_____Reviewed

By: _____, _____

Time : _____ Classification: _____ Processing Applied? No ___ Yes ___ (Type) _____

Transcript :

_____

_____

Any external stimuli applied? No ____ Yes ____ (Type)

_____

_____

Leading Questions or Conversation

_____

_____

Any other sounds recorded?

_____Reviewed

By: _____, _____

1

REPORTING INVESTIGATOR NAME OR NUMBER:_____

~ EVP Log Book ~

URN: _____ , _____ , _____ - _____ - _____

Day Month Year Number Type

Location :

_____

Investigating Team : _____

_____

_____

_____

_____

Set Up Sheet - Hardware Configuration

Audio Equipment ----- _____

_____

_____

_____

_____

Support Equipment -- _____.

_____

_____

Sources of Interaction - _____

_____

_____

Audio Equipment ----- _____

_____

_____

_____

Support Equipment -- _____

_____

_____

_____

Sources of Interaction - _____

_____

_____

_____

3___

Layout of Target Area - (Sketch Below)

Real Time Event Log 4___
Line Time Event Witnessed

_____ - _____ -
_____
_____ - _____

_____ - _____ -
_____
_____ - _____

_____ - _____ -
_____
_____ - _____

_____ - _____ -
_____
_____ - _____

_____ - _____ -
_____
_____ - _____

_____ - _____ -
_____
_____ - _____

_____ - _____ -
_____
_____ - _____

Quality Grading: (EVP Research Standards)

- o **A_** Heard and understood clearly without any signal processing at all, Like a normal voice.
- o **B_** Processed using analog filtering, but most who hear it can decipher the content. There is little disagreement on what is recorded.
- o **C_** Processed using analog filtering, but still hard to hear. Potential for disagreement on content.
- o **D_** Digital processing employed to make out anything at all. Disagreement over content, some may not hear anything.
- o **E_** Most hear nothing; some may claim to hear a voice. Processing may result in different messages being heard.

Content Grading

- o **1_** Easily related to surroundings. For instance: A soldier who was killed mentioning the battle, etc.
- o **2_** Unrelated but meaningful, such as a statement "I love you". Could be for anyone or maybe no one present.
- o **3_** Gibberish. Meaningless groups of words but still recognizable as words or phrases.
- o **4_** Utterances. Vocalized sounds not words. Includes grunts and groans. Before classifying here make sure you are not dealing with a foreign language which should actually be in categories 1-3.
- o **5_** Non vocal sounds. Thumps Bangs, Pops, Footsteps, etc.

Source Grading: 5

- o **M_** Multiple voices heard, unable to differentiate.
- o **U_** The gender or age cannot be determined.
- o **W_** The voice is clearly that of a child.
- o **X_** The voice is clearly that of a woman.
- o **Y_** The voice is clearly that of a man.
- o **Z_** The recording is of an animal sound (Barking, Meowing, Vocalizations only)

- Note that many EVPs may contain portions falling into multiple categories. Parts may be clear then fade out. Vocalizations may be preceded or followed by non-vocal sounds. Thus a particular EVP may have multiple classifications. If you are classifying the overall EVP, use the most predominate characteristics.

To Grade your EVP, select the appropriate **letter** from the first column, **number** from the second column and finally **letter** from the third. Enter that grading under the "Classification" on the Post Investigation Summary Sheet.

Post Investigation Summary Sheet 6__

Time : _____ Classification: _____ Processing Applied? No
___ Yes ___ (Type) _____

Transcript :
_____
_____

Any external stimuli applied? No _____ Yes _____ (Type)
_____
_____

Leading Questions or Conversation
_____
_____

Any other sounds recorded?
_____Reviewed
By: _____, _____

Time : _____ Classification: _____ Processing Applied? No
___ Yes ___ (Type) _____

Transcript :
_____
_____

Any external stimuli applied? No _____ Yes _____ (Type)
_____
_____

Leading Questions or Conversation
_____
_____

Any other sounds recorded?
_____Reviewed
By: _____, _____

Time : _____ Classification: _____ Processing Applied? No
___ Yes ___ (Type) _____

Transcript :
_____
_____

Any external stimuli applied? No _____ Yes _____ (Type)
_____
_____

Leading Questions or Conversation
_____
_____

Any other sounds recorded?
_____Reviewed
By: _____, _____

REPORTING INVESTIGATOR NAME OR NUMBER:_____

~ EVP Log Book ~

URN: _____ , _____ , _____ - _____ - _____

Day Month Year Number Type

Location :

_____

Investigating Team : _____

_____

_____

_____

_____

Set Up Sheet - Hardware Configuration

Audio Equipment ----- _____

_____

_____

_____

Support Equipment -- _____

_____

_____

Sources of Interaction - _____

_____

_____

Audio Equipment ----- _____

_____

_____

_____

Support Equipment -- _____

_____

_____

_____

Sources of Interaction - _____

_____

_____

_____

3___

Layout of Target Area - (Sketch Below)

Real Time Event Log 4___
Line Time Event Witnessed

_____ - _____ -

_____

_____ - _____

_____ - _____ -

_____

_____ - _____

_____ - _____ -

_____

_____ - _____

_____ - _____ -

_____

_____ - _____

_____ - _____ -

_____

_____ - _____

_____ - _____ -

_____

_____ - _____

_____ - _____ -

_____

_____ - _____

Quality Grading: (EVP Research Standards)

- **A_** Heard and understood clearly without any signal processing at all, Like a normal voice.
- **B_** Processed using analog filtering, but most who hear it can decipher the content. There is little disagreement on what is recorded.
- **C_** Processed using analog filtering, but still hard to hear. Potential for disagreement on content.
- **D_** Digital processing employed to make out anything at all. Disagreement over content, some may not hear anything.
- **E_** Most hear nothing; some may claim to hear a voice. Processing may result in different messages being heard.

Content Grading

- **1_** Easily related to surroundings. For instance: A soldier who was killed mentioning the battle, etc.
- **2_** Unrelated but meaningful, such as a statement "I love you". Could be for anyone or maybe no one present.
- **3_** Gibberish. Meaningless groups of words but still recognizable as words or phrases.
- **4_** Utterances. Vocalized sounds not words. Includes grunts and groans. Before classifying here make sure you are not dealing with a foreign language which should actually be in categories 1-3.
- **5_** Non vocal sounds. Thumps Bangs, Pops, Footsteps, etc.

Source Grading: 5

- **M_** Multiple voices heard, unable to differentiate.
- **U_** The gender or age cannot be determined.
- **W_** The voice is clearly that of a child.
- **X_** The voice is clearly that of a woman.
- **Y_** The voice is clearly that of a man.
- **Z_** The recording is of an animal sound (Barking, Meowing, Vocalizations only)

- Note that many EVPs may contain portions falling into multiple categories. Parts may be clear then fade out. Vocalizations may be preceded or followed by non-vocal sounds. Thus a particular EVP may have multiple classifications. If you are classifying the overall EVP, use the most predominate characteristics.

To Grade your EVP, select the appropriate **letter** from the first column, **number** from the second column and finally **letter** from the third. Enter that grading under the "Classification" on the Post Investigation Summary Sheet.

Post Investigation Summary Sheet 6__

Time : _____ Classification: _____ Processing Applied? No ___ Yes ___ (Type) _____

Transcript :
_____
_____

Any external stimuli applied? No _____ Yes _____ (Type)
_____
_____

Leading Questions or Conversation
_____
_____

Any other sounds recorded?
_____Reviewed
By: _____, _____

Time : _____ Classification: _____ Processing Applied? No
___ Yes ___ (Type) _____

Transcript :
_____
_____

Any external stimuli applied? No ____ Yes ____ (Type)
_____
_____

Leading Questions or Conversation
_____
_____

Any other sounds recorded?
_____Reviewed
By: _____, _____

Time : _____ Classification: _____ Processing Applied? No
___ Yes ___ (Type) _____

Transcript :
_____
_____

Any external stimuli applied? No ____ Yes ____ (Type)
_____
_____

Leading Questions or Conversation
_____
_____

Any other sounds recorded?
_____Reviewed
By: _____, _____

REPORTING INVESTIGATOR NAME OR NUMBER:_____

~ EVP Log Book ~

URN: _____ , _____ , _____ - _____ - _____

Day Month Year Number Type

Location :

_____

Investigating Team : _____

_____

_____

_____

_____

Set Up Sheet - Hardware Configuration

Audio Equipment ----- _____

_____

_____

_____

_____

Support Equipment -- _____

_____

_____

Sources of Interaction - _____

_____

_____

Audio Equipment ----- _____

_____

_____

_____

Support Equipment -- _____

_____

_____

_____

Sources of Interaction - _____

_____

_____

_____

3___

Layout of Target Area - (Sketch Below)

Real Time Event Log 4___
Line Time Event Witnessed

_____ - _____ - _____

_____

_____ - _____

_____ - _____ - _____

_____

_____ - _____

_____ - _____ - _____

_____

_____ - _____

_____ - _____ - _____

_____

_____ - _____

_____ - _____ - _____

_____

_____ - _____

_____ - _____ - _____

_____

_____ - _____

_____ - _____ - _____

_____

_____ - _____

Quality Grading: (EVP Research Standards)

- **A_** Heard and understood clearly without any signal processing at all, Like a normal voice.
- **B_** Processed using analog filtering, but most who hear it can decipher the content. There is little disagreement on what is recorded.
- **C_** Processed using analog filtering, but still hard to hear. Potential for disagreement on content.
- **D_** Digital processing employed to make out anything at all. Disagreement over content, some may not hear anything.
- **E_** Most hear nothing; some may claim to hear a voice. Processing may result in different messages being heard.

Content Grading

- **1_** Easily related to surroundings. For instance: A soldier who was killed mentioning the battle, etc.
- **2_** Unrelated but meaningful, such as a statement "I love you". Could be for anyone or maybe no one present.
- **3_** Gibberish. Meaningless groups of words but still recognizable as words or phrases.
- **4_** Utterances. Vocalized sounds not words. Includes grunts and groans. Before classifying here make sure you are not dealing with a foreign language which should actually be in categories 1-3.
- **5_** Non vocal sounds. Thumps Bangs, Pops, Footsteps, etc.

Source Grading: 5

- **M_** Multiple voices heard, unable to differentiate.
- **U_** The gender or age cannot be determined.
- **W_** The voice is clearly that of a child.
- **X_** The voice is clearly that of a woman.
- **Y_** The voice is clearly that of a man.
- **Z_** The recording is of an animal sound (Barking, Meowing, Vocalizations only)

- Note that many EVPs may contain portions falling into multiple categories. Parts may be clear then fade out. Vocalizations may be preceded or followed by non-vocal sounds. Thus a particular EVP may have multiple classifications. If you are classifying the overall EVP, use the most predominate characteristics.

To Grade your EVP, select the appropriate **letter** from the first column, **number** from the second column and finally **letter** from the third. Enter that grading under the "Classification" on the Post Investigation Summary Sheet.

Post Investigation Summary Sheet 6__

Time : _____ Classification: _____ Processing Applied? No ___ Yes ___ (Type) _____

Transcript :
_____
_____

Any external stimuli applied? No _____ Yes _____ (Type)
_____
_____

Leading Questions or Conversation
_____
_____

Any other sounds recorded?
_____Reviewed
By: _____, _____

Time : _____ Classification: _____ Processing Applied? No
___ Yes ___ (Type) _____

Transcript :
_____
_____

Any external stimuli applied? No ____ Yes ____ (Type)
_____
_____

Leading Questions or Conversation
_____
_____

Any other sounds recorded?
_____Reviewed
By: _____, _____

Time : _____ Classification: _____ Processing Applied? No
___ Yes ___ (Type) _____

Transcript :
_____
_____

Any external stimuli applied? No ____ Yes ____ (Type)
_____
_____

Leading Questions or Conversation
_____
_____

Any other sounds recorded?
_____Reviewed
By: _____, _____

1

REPORTING INVESTIGATOR NAME OR
NUMBER:_____

~ EVP Log Book ~

URN: _____ , _____ , _____ - _____ - _____

Day Month Year Number Type

Location :

_____

Investigating Team : _____

_____

_____

_____

_____

Set Up Sheet - Hardware Configuration

Audio Equipment ----- _____

_____

_____

_____

Support Equipment -- _____

_____

_____

Sources of Interaction - _____

_____

_____

Audio Equipment ----- _____

_____

_____

_____

Support Equipment -- _____

_____

_____

_____

Sources of Interaction - _____

_____

_____

_____

3___

Layout of Target Area - (Sketch Below)

Real Time Event Log 4___
Line Time Event Witnessed

_____ - _____ - ___

_____

_____ - _____

_____ - _____ - ___

_____

_____ - _____ -

_____ - _____ - ___

_____

_____ - _____ -

_____ - _____ - ___

_____

_____ - _____ -

_____ - _____ - ___

_____

_____ - _____ -

_____ - _____ - ___

_____

_____ - _____ -

_____ - _____ - ___

_____

_____ - _____ -

_____ - _____ - ___

_____

_____ - _____

_____ - _____ - ___

_____

_____ - _____

Quality Grading: (EVP Research Standards)

- **A_** Heard and understood clearly without any signal processing at all, Like a normal voice.
- **B_** Processed using analog filtering, but most who hear it can decipher the content. There is little disagreement on what is recorded.
- **C_** Processed using analog filtering, but still hard to hear. Potential for disagreement on content.
- **D_** Digital processing employed to make out anything at all. Disagreement over content, some may not hear anything.
- **E_** Most hear nothing; some may claim to hear a voice. Processing may result in different messages being heard.

Content Grading

- **1_** Easily related to surroundings. For instance: A soldier who was killed mentioning the battle, etc.
- **2_** Unrelated but meaningful, such as a statement "I love you". Could be for anyone or maybe no one present.
- **3_** Gibberish. Meaningless groups of words but still recognizable as words or phrases.
- **4_** Utterances. Vocalized sounds not words. Includes grunts and groans. Before classifying here make sure you are not dealing with a foreign language which should actually be in categories 1-3.
- **5_** Non vocal sounds. Thumps Bangs, Pops, Footsteps, etc.

Source Grading: 5

- **M_** Multiple voices heard, unable to differentiate.
- **U_** The gender or age cannot be determined.
- **W_** The voice is clearly that of a child.
- **X_** The voice is clearly that of a woman.
- **Y_** The voice is clearly that of a man.
- **Z_** The recording is of an animal sound (Barking, Meowing, Vocalizations only)

- Note that many EVPs may contain portions falling into multiple categories. Parts may be clear then fade out. Vocalizations may be preceded or followed by non-vocal sounds. Thus a particular EVP may have multiple classifications. If you are classifying the overall EVP, use the most predominate characteristics.

To Grade your EVP, select the appropriate **letter** from the first column, **number** from the second column and finally **letter** from the third. Enter that grading under the "Classification" on the Post Investigation Summary Sheet.

Post Investigation Summary Sheet 6__

Time : _____ Classification: _____ Processing Applied? No ____ Yes ___ (Type) _____

Transcript :

_____

_____

Any external stimuli applied? No _____ Yes _____ (Type)

_____

_____

Leading Questions or Conversation

_____

_____

Any other sounds recorded?

_____Reviewed

By: _____, _____

Time : _____ Classification: _____ Processing Applied? No
___ Yes ___ (Type) _____

Transcript :

_____
_____

Any external stimuli applied? No _____ Yes _____ (Type)

_____
_____

Leading Questions or Conversation

_____
_____

Any other sounds recorded?

_____Reviewed
By: _____, _____

Time : _____ Classification: _____ Processing Applied? No
___ Yes ___ (Type) _____

Transcript :

_____
_____

Any external stimuli applied? No _____ Yes _____ (Type)

_____
_____

Leading Questions or Conversation

_____
_____

Any other sounds recorded?

_____Reviewed
By: _____, _____

1

REPORTING INVESTIGATOR NAME OR
NUMBER:_____

~ EVP Log Book ~

URN: _____ , _____ , _____ - _____ - _____

Day Month Year Number Type

Location :
_____

Investigating Team : _____

_____

_____

_____

_____

Set Up Sheet - Hardware Configuration

Audio Equipment ----- _____

_____

_____

_____

_____

Support Equipment -- _____

_____

_____

Sources of Interaction - _____

_____

_____

Audio Equipment ----- _____

_____

_____

_____

Support Equipment -- _____

_____

_____

_____

Sources of Interaction - _____

_____

_____

_____

3___

Layout of Target Area - (Sketch Below)

Real Time Event Log 4___
Line Time Event Witnessed

_____ - _____ -

_____

_____ - _____

_____ - _____ -

_____ - _____

_____ - _____ -

_____

_____ - _____

_____ - _____ -

_____

_____ - _____

_____ - _____ -

_____ - _____

_____ - _____ -

_____

_____ - _____

_____ - _____ -

_____

_____ - _____

_____ - _____ -

_____

_____ - _____

Quality Grading: (EVP Research Standards)

- **A_** Heard and understood clearly without any signal processing at all, Like a normal voice.
- **B_** Processed using analog filtering, but most who hear it can decipher the content. There is little disagreement on what is recorded.
- **C_** Processed using analog filtering, but still hard to hear. Potential for disagreement on content.
- **D_** Digital processing employed to make out anything at all. Disagreement over content, some may not hear anything.
- **E_** Most hear nothing; some may claim to hear a voice. Processing may result in different messages being heard.

Content Grading

- **1_** Easily related to surroundings. For instance: A soldier who was killed mentioning the battle, etc.
- **2_** Unrelated but meaningful, such as a statement "I love you". Could be for anyone or maybe no one present.
- **3_** Gibberish. Meaningless groups of words but still recognizable as words or phrases.
- **4_** Utterances. Vocalized sounds not words. Includes grunts and groans. Before classifying here make sure you are not dealing with a foreign language which should actually be in categories 1-3.
- **5_** Non vocal sounds. Thumps Bangs, Pops, Footsteps, etc.

Source Grading: 5

- **M_** Multiple voices heard, unable to differentiate.
- **U_** The gender or age cannot be determined.
- **W_** The voice is clearly that of a child.
- **X_** The voice is clearly that of a woman.
- **Y_** The voice is clearly that of a man.
- **Z_** The recording is of an animal sound (Barking, Meowing, Vocalizations only)

- Note that many EVPs may contain portions falling into multiple categories. Parts may be clear then fade out. Vocalizations may be preceded or followed by non-vocal sounds. Thus a particular EVP may have multiple classifications. If you are classifying the overall EVP, use the most predominate characteristics.

To Grade your EVP, select the appropriate **letter** from the first column, **number** from the second column and finally **letter** from the third. Enter that grading under the "Classification" on the Post Investigation Summary Sheet.

Post Investigation Summary Sheet 6__

Time : _____ Classification: _____ Processing Applied? No
___ Yes ___ (Type) _____

Transcript :
_____
_____

Any external stimuli applied? No ____ **Yes** ____ **(Type)**
_____
_____

Leading Questions or Conversation
_____
_____

Any other sounds recorded?
_____**Reviewed**
By: _____ , _____

Time : _____ **Classification:** _____ **Processing Applied? No** ___ **Yes** ___ **(Type)** _____

Transcript :
_____
_____

Any external stimuli applied? No ____ **Yes** ____ **(Type)**
_____
_____

Leading Questions or Conversation
_____
_____

Any other sounds recorded?
_____**Reviewed**
By: _____, _____

Time : _____ **Classification:** _____ **Processing Applied? No** ___ **Yes** ___ **(Type)** _____

Transcript :
_____
_____

Any external stimuli applied? No ____ **Yes** ____ **(Type)**
_____
_____

Leading Questions or Conversation
_____
_____

Any other sounds recorded?
_____**Reviewed**
By: _____, _____

REPORTING INVESTIGATOR NAME OR NUMBER:_____

~ EVP Log Book ~

URN: _____ , _____ , _____ - _____ - _____

Day Month Year Number Type

Location :

_____

Investigating Team : _____

_____

_____

_____

_____

Set Up Sheet - Hardware Configuration

Audio Equipment ----- _____

_____

_____

_____

_____

Support Equipment -- _____

_____

_____

Sources of Interaction - _____

_____

_____

Audio Equipment ----- _____

_____

_____

_____

Support Equipment -- _____

_____

_____

_____

Sources of Interaction - _____

_____

_____

_____

3___

Layout of Target Area - (Sketch Below)

Real Time Event Log 4___
Line Time Event Witnessed

Quality Grading: (EVP Research Standards)

- **A_** Heard and understood clearly without any signal processing at all, Like a normal voice.
- **B_** Processed using analog filtering, but most who hear it can decipher the content. There is little disagreement on what is recorded.
- **C_** Processed using analog filtering, but still hard to hear. Potential for disagreement on content.
- **D_** Digital processing employed to make out anything at all. Disagreement over content, some may not hear anything.
- **E_** Most hear nothing; some may claim to hear a voice. Processing may result in different messages being heard.

Content Grading

- **1_** Easily related to surroundings. For instance: A soldier who was killed mentioning the battle, etc.
- **2_** Unrelated but meaningful, such as a statement "I love you". Could be for anyone or maybe no one present.
- **3_** Gibberish. Meaningless groups of words but still recognizable as words or phrases.
- **4_** Utterances. Vocalized sounds not words. Includes grunts and groans. Before classifying here make sure you are not dealing with a foreign language which should actually be in categories 1-3.
- **5_** Non vocal sounds. Thumps Bangs, Pops, Footsteps, etc.

Source Grading: 5

- **M_** Multiple voices heard, unable to differentiate.
- **U_** The gender or age cannot be determined.
- **W_** The voice is clearly that of a child.
- **X_** The voice is clearly that of a woman.
- **Y_** The voice is clearly that of a man.
- **Z_** The recording is of an animal sound (Barking, Meowing, Vocalizations only)

- Note that many EVPs may contain portions falling into multiple categories. Parts may be clear then fade out. Vocalizations may be preceded or followed by non-vocal sounds. Thus a particular EVP may have multiple classifications. If you are classifying the overall EVP, use the most predominate characteristics.

To Grade your EVP, select the appropriate **letter** from the first column, **number** from the second column and finally **letter** from the third. Enter that grading under the "Classification" on the Post Investigation Summary Sheet.

Post Investigation Summary Sheet 6__

Time : _____ Classification: _____ Processing Applied? No ___ Yes ___ (Type) _____

Transcript :

_____

_____

Any external stimuli applied? No ____ Yes ____ (Type)

_____

_____

Leading Questions or Conversation

_____

_____

Any other sounds recorded?

_____Reviewed
By: _____, _____

Time : _____ Classification: _____ Processing Applied? No
___ Yes ___ (Type) _____ ____

Transcript :

_____
_____

Any external stimuli applied? No _____ Yes _____ (Type)

_____
_____

Leading Questions or Conversation

_____
_____

Any other sounds recorded?

_____Reviewed
By: _____, _____

Time : _____ Classification: _____ Processing Applied? No
___ Yes ___ (Type) _____

Transcript :

_____
_____

Any external stimuli applied? No _____ Yes _____ (Type)

_____
_____

Leading Questions or Conversation

_____
_____

Any other sounds recorded?

_____Reviewed
By: _____, _____

REPORTING INVESTIGATOR NAME OR
NUMBER:_____

~ EVP Log Book ~

URN: _____ , _____ , _____ - _____ - _____

Day Month Year Number Type

Location :

_____

Investigating Team : _____

_____

_____

_____

_____

Set Up Sheet - Hardware Configuration

Audio Equipment ----- _____

_____

_____

_____

_____

Support Equipment -- _____

_____

_____

Sources of Interaction - _____

_____

_____

Audio Equipment ----- _____

_____

_____

_____

Support Equipment -- _____

_____

_____

_____

Sources of Interaction - _____

_____

_____

_____

3___

Layout of Target Area - (Sketch Below)

Real Time Event Log 4___
Line Time Event Witnessed

_____ - _____ -
_____
_____ - _____

_____ - _____ -
_____
_____ - _____

_____ - _____ -
_____
_____ - _____

_____ - _____ -
_____
_____ - _____

_____ - _____ -
_____
_____ - _____

_____ - _____ -
_____
_____ - _____

_____ - _____ -
_____
_____ - _____

Quality Grading: (EVP Research Standards)

- o **A_** Heard and understood clearly without any signal processing at all, Like a normal voice.
- o **B_** Processed using analog filtering, but most who hear it can decipher the content. There is little disagreement on what is recorded.
- o **C_** Processed using analog filtering, but still hard to hear. Potential for disagreement on content.
- o **D_** Digital processing employed to make out anything at all. Disagreement over content, some may not hear anything.
- o **E_** Most hear nothing; some may claim to hear a voice. Processing may result in different messages being heard.

Content Grading

- o **1_** Easily related to surroundings. For instance: A soldier who was killed mentioning the battle, etc.
- o **2_** Unrelated but meaningful, such as a statement "I love you". Could be for anyone or maybe no one present.
- o **3_** Gibberish. Meaningless groups of words but still recognizable as words or phrases.
- o **4_** Utterances. Vocalized sounds not words. Includes grunts and groans. Before classifying here make sure you are not dealing with a foreign language which should actually be in categories 1-3.
- o **5_** Non vocal sounds. Thumps Bangs, Pops, Footsteps, etc.

Source Grading: 5

- o **M_** Multiple voices heard, unable to differentiate.
- o **U_** The gender or age cannot be determined.
- o **W_** The voice is clearly that of a child.
- o **X_** The voice is clearly that of a woman.
- o **Y_** The voice is clearly that of a man.
- o **Z_** The recording is of an animal sound (Barking, Meowing, Vocalizations only)

- Note that many EVPs may contain portions falling into multiple categories. Parts may be clear then fade out. Vocalizations may be preceded or followed by non-vocal sounds. Thus a particular EVP may have multiple classifications. If you are classifying the overall EVP, use the most predominate characteristics.

To Grade your EVP, select the appropriate **letter** from the first column, **number** from the second column and finally **letter** from the third. Enter that grading under the "Classification" on the Post Investigation Summary Sheet.

Post Investigation Summary Sheet 6__

Time : _____ **Classification:** _____ **Processing Applied? No** ___ **Yes** ___ **(Type)** _____

Transcript :
_____
_____

Any external stimuli applied? No _____ **Yes** _____ **(Type)**
_____
_____

Leading Questions or Conversation
_____
_____

Any other sounds recorded?
_____**Reviewed**
By: _____, _____

Time : _____ Classification: _____ Processing Applied? No ___ Yes ___ (Type) _____

Transcript :
_____
_____

Any external stimuli applied? No _____ Yes _____ (Type)
_____
_____

Leading Questions or Conversation
_____
_____

Any other sounds recorded?
_____Reviewed
By: _____, _____

Time : _____ Classification: _____ Processing Applied? No ___ Yes ___ (Type) _____

Transcript :
_____
_____

Any external stimuli applied? No _____ Yes _____ (Type)
_____
_____

Leading Questions or Conversation
_____
_____

Any other sounds recorded?
_____Reviewed
By: _____, _____

**REPORTING INVESTIGATOR NAME OR
NUMBER:**_____

~ EVP Log Book ~

URN: _____ , _____ , _____ - _____ - _____

Day Month Year Number Type

Location :

_____

Investigating Team : _____

_____

_____

_____

_____

Set Up Sheet - Hardware Configuration

Audio Equipment ----- _____

_____

_____

_____

_____

Support Equipment -- _____

_____

_____

Sources of Interaction - _____

_____

_____

Audio Equipment ----- _____

_____

_____

_____

Support Equipment -- _____

_____

_____

_____

Sources of Interaction - _____

_____

_____

_____

3___

Layout of Target Area - (Sketch Below)

Real Time Event Log 4___
Line Time Event Witnessed

_____ - _____ -
_____

_____ - _____

_____ - _____ -
_____

_____ - _____

_____ - _____ -
_____

_____ - _____

_____ - _____ -
_____

_____ - _____

_____ - _____ -
_____

_____ - _____

_____ - _____ -
_____

_____ - _____

_____ - _____ -
_____

_____ - _____

_____ - _____ -
_____

_____ - _____

Quality Grading: (EVP Research Standards)

- o **A_** Heard and understood clearly without any signal processing at all, Like a normal voice.
- o **B_** Processed using analog filtering, but most who hear it can decipher the content. There is little disagreement on what is recorded.
- o **C_** Processed using analog filtering, but still hard to hear. Potential for disagreement on content.
- o **D_** Digital processing employed to make out anything at all. Disagreement over content, some may not hear anything.
- o **E_** Most hear nothing; some may claim to hear a voice. Processing may result in different messages being heard.

Content Grading

- o **1_** Easily related to surroundings. For instance: A soldier who was killed mentioning the battle, etc.
- o **2_** Unrelated but meaningful, such as a statement "I love you". Could be for anyone or maybe no one present.
- o **3_** Gibberish. Meaningless groups of words but still recognizable as words or phrases.
- o **4_** Utterances. Vocalized sounds not words. Includes grunts and groans. Before classifying here make sure you are not dealing with a foreign language which should actually be in categories 1-3.
- o **5_** Non vocal sounds. Thumps Bangs, Pops, Footsteps, etc.

Source Grading: 5

- o **M_** Multiple voices heard, unable to differentiate.
- o **U_** The gender or age cannot be determined.
- o **W_** The voice is clearly that of a child.
- o **X_** The voice is clearly that of a woman.
- o **Y_** The voice is clearly that of a man.
- o **Z_** The recording is of an animal sound (Barking, Meowing, Vocalizations only)

- Note that many EVPs may contain portions falling into multiple categories. Parts may be clear then fade out. Vocalizations may be preceded or followed by non-vocal sounds. Thus a particular EVP may have multiple classifications. If you are classifying the overall EVP, use the most predominate characteristics.

To Grade your EVP, select the appropriate **letter** from the first column, **number** from the second column and finally **letter** from the third. Enter that grading under the "Classification" on the Post Investigation Summary Sheet.

Post Investigation Summary Sheet 6__

Time : _____ **Classification:** _____ **Processing Applied? No** ___ **Yes** ___ **(Type)** _____

Transcript :
_____
_____

Any external stimuli applied? No _____ **Yes** _____ **(Type)**
_____
_____

Leading Questions or Conversation
_____
_____

Any other sounds recorded?
_____**Reviewed**
By: _____, _____

Time : _____ **Classification:** _____ **Processing Applied? No**
___ **Yes** ___ **(Type)** _____ ____

Transcript :

_____
_____

Any external stimuli applied? No _____ **Yes** _____ **(Type)**

_____
_____

Leading Questions or Conversation

_____
_____

Any other sounds recorded?
_____**Reviewed**
By: _____, _____

Time : _____ **Classification:** _____ **Processing Applied? No**
___ **Yes** ___ **(Type)** _____

Transcript :

_____
_____

Any external stimuli applied? No _____ **Yes** _____ **(Type)**

_____
_____.

Leading Questions or Conversation

_____
_____

Any other sounds recorded?
_____**Reviewed**
By: _____, _____

1

REPORTING INVESTIGATOR NAME OR
NUMBER:_____

~ EVP Log Book ~

URN: _____ , _____ , _____ - _____ - _____

Day Month Year Number Type

Location :
_____

Investigating Team : _____

_____

_____

_____

_____

Set Up Sheet - Hardware Configuration

Audio Equipment ----- _____

_____

_____

_____

Support Equipment -- _____

_____

_____

Sources of Interaction - _____

_____

_____

Audio Equipment ----- _____

_____

_____

_____

Support Equipment -- _____

_____

_____

_____

Sources of Interaction - _____

_____

_____

_____

3___

Layout of Target Area - (Sketch Below)

Real Time Event Log 4___
Line Time Event Witnessed

_____ - _____ - _____

_____

_____ - _____

_____ - _____ - _____

_____

_____ - _____

_____ - _____ - _____

_____

_____ - _____

_____ - _____ - _____

_____

_____ - _____

_____ - _____ - _____

_____

_____ - _____

_____ - _____ - _____

_____

_____ - _____

_____ - _____ - _____

_____

_____ - _____

_____ - _____ - _____

_____

_____ - _____

_____ - _____ - _____

_____

_____ - _____

Quality Grading: (EVP Research Standards)

- **A_** Heard and understood clearly without any signal processing at all, Like a normal voice.
- **B_** Processed using analog filtering, but most who hear it can decipher the content. There is little disagreement on what is recorded.
- **C_** Processed using analog filtering, but still hard to hear. Potential for disagreement on content.
- **D_** Digital processing employed to make out anything at all. Disagreement over content, some may not hear anything.
- **E_** Most hear nothing; some may claim to hear a voice. Processing may result in different messages being heard.

Content Grading

- **1_** Easily related to surroundings. For instance: A soldier who was killed mentioning the battle, etc.
- **2_** Unrelated but meaningful, such as a statement "I love you". Could be for anyone or maybe no one present.
- **3_** Gibberish. Meaningless groups of words but still recognizable as words or phrases.
- **4_** Utterances. Vocalized sounds not words. Includes grunts and groans. Before classifying here make sure you are not dealing with a foreign language which should actually be in categories 1-3.
- **5_** Non vocal sounds. Thumps Bangs, Pops, Footsteps, etc.

Source Grading: 5

- **M_** Multiple voices heard, unable to differentiate.
- **U_** The gender or age cannot be determined.
- **W_** The voice is clearly that of a child.
- **X_** The voice is clearly that of a woman.
- **Y_** The voice is clearly that of a man.
- **Z_** The recording is of an animal sound (Barking, Meowing, Vocalizations only)

- Note that many EVPs may contain portions falling into multiple categories. Parts may be clear then fade out. Vocalizations may be preceded or followed by non-vocal sounds. Thus a particular EVP may have multiple classifications. If you are classifying the overall EVP, use the most predominate characteristics.

To Grade your EVP, select the appropriate **letter** from the first column, **number** from the second column and finally **letter** from the third. Enter that grading under the "Classification" on the Post Investigation Summary Sheet.

Post Investigation Summary Sheet 6__

Time : _____ Classification: _____ Processing Applied? No ___ Yes ___ (Type) _____

Transcript :
_____
_____

Any external stimuli applied? No _____ Yes _____ (Type)
_____
_____

Leading Questions or Conversation
_____
_____

Any other sounds recorded?
_____Reviewed
By: _____, _____

Time : _____ Classification: _____ Processing Applied? No
___ Yes ___ (Type) _____

Transcript :

_____
_____

Any external stimuli applied? No ____ Yes ____ (Type)

_____
_____

Leading Questions or Conversation

_____
_____

Any other sounds recorded?

_____Reviewed
By: _____, _____

Time : _____ Classification: _____ Processing Applied? No
___ Yes ___ (Type) _____

Transcript :

_____
_____

Any external stimuli applied? No ____ Yes ____ (Type)

_____
_____

Leading Questions or Conversation

_____
_____

Any other sounds recorded?

_____Reviewed
By: _____, _____

Thank you for Using Project-reveal to help with your paranormal ghost
hunting Findings
www.project-reveal.com
www.facebook.com/facebook

CPSIA information can be obtained
at www.ICGtesting.com
Printed in the USA
FFOW01n1422211216
30656FF

9 781481 286363